THE SOLAR SYSTEM

Text by
Beatrice McLeod

Illustrations by
Lorenzo Cecchi

M^cRAE BOOKS

THE GALAXY

Galaxies can be elliptical (oval), spiral, or irregular in shape. Our galaxy is shaped like a spiral. It has a dense central disk and four great arms of stars surrounded by a less dense halo. The Solar System lies about two-thirds out along the Orion Arm of the Galaxy.

Sagittarius arm

Crux-Centaurus arm / *Orion arm*

Central disk

You are here

Perseus arm

FORMATION OF THE SOLAR SYSTEM

The Solar System was formed from a cloud of gas and dust about 4.6 billion years ago.

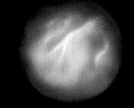

Cloud of dust and gas.

Protostar gradually forms at the center.

Planets form and begin to orbit around the Sun.

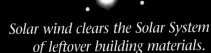

Solar wind clears the Solar System of leftover building materials.

THE GALAXY

Our Galaxy, which is called the Milky Way, is vast. It measures about 100,000 light years across – a light year is about 5,912 billion miles (9,460 billion km). In comparison, the Solar System is only about 12 light hours across. The Galaxy is shaped like a spiral, with a central disk and four huge arms of stars uncoiling outward into space. All the matter in the Galaxy rotates around its center. The Solar System lies in the Orion Arm (also called the Local Arm) of the Galaxy. The Sun, which is located at the center of our Solar System, is just one of about 200 billion stars in the Milky Way Galaxy. It takes about 230 million years for the Sun to complete a revolution of the Galaxy.

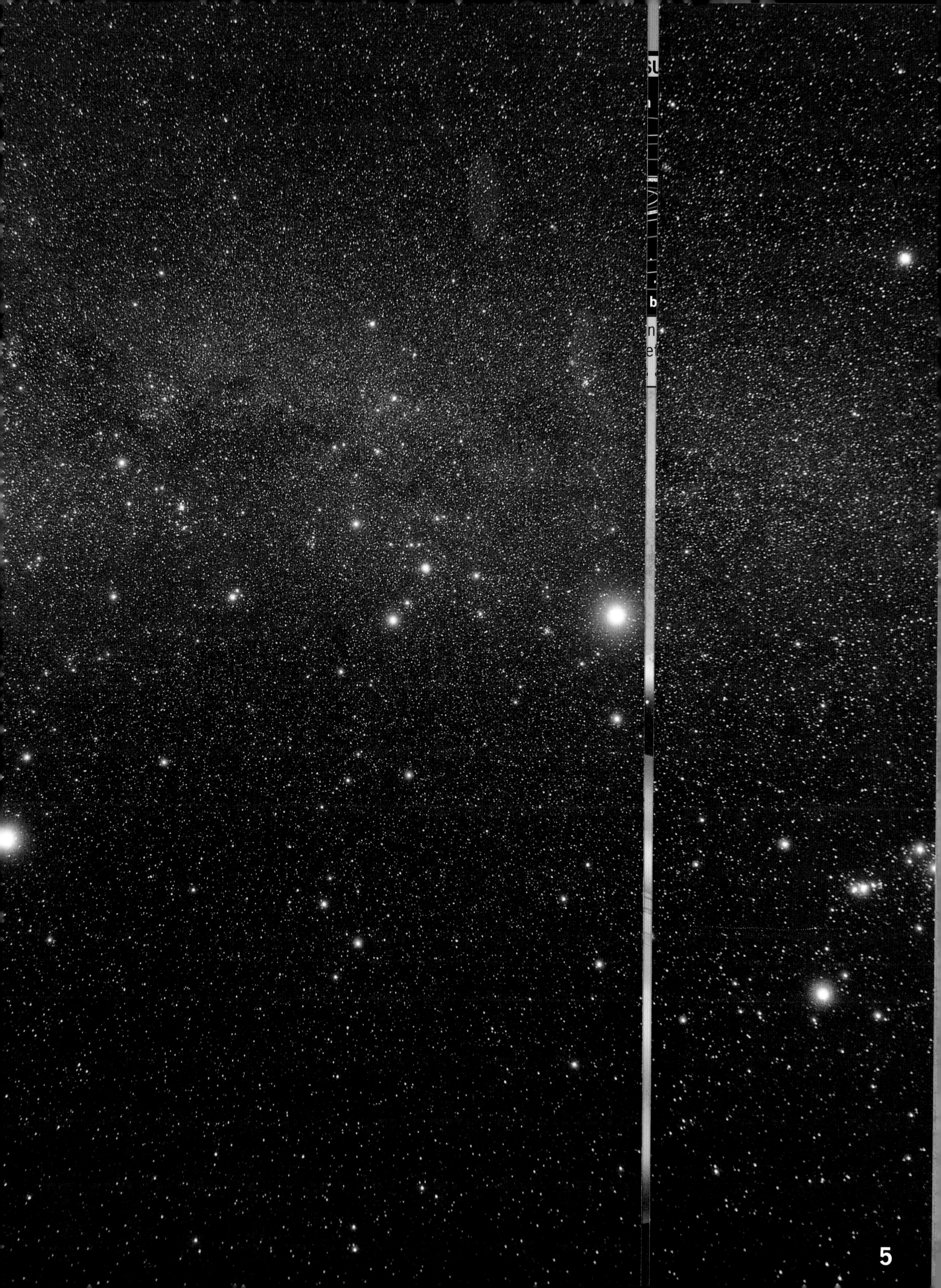

The Sun formed when a cloud of gas and dust contracted under the pull of its own gravity. As the cloud shrank it became hotter and hotter. When the temperature at the core reached about 27 million °F (15 million °C), nuclear reactions began to generate large amounts of energy and the Sun began to shine.

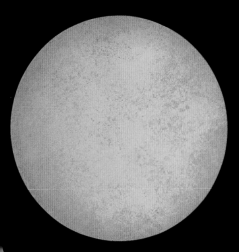

Sun

The Sun is now a main sequence star. In about 5 billion years it will become a Red Giant, and finally, a White Dwarf. Some more massive stars become Red Supergiants and then very dense Neutron Stars or Black Holes.

Red Giant

- *White Dwarf*
- *Neutron Star*
  Black Hole

THE SUN

The Sun is the star at the center of our Solar System. Measuring 865,000 miles (1,392,000 km) in diameter, it has about 330,000 times the mass of the Earth. It dwarfs everything else in the Solar System. If the Sun were a soccer ball, the Earth would be smaller than a pea in comparison. A huge, dynamic ball of gas, the Sun provides the light and heat that allows life to exist on Earth.

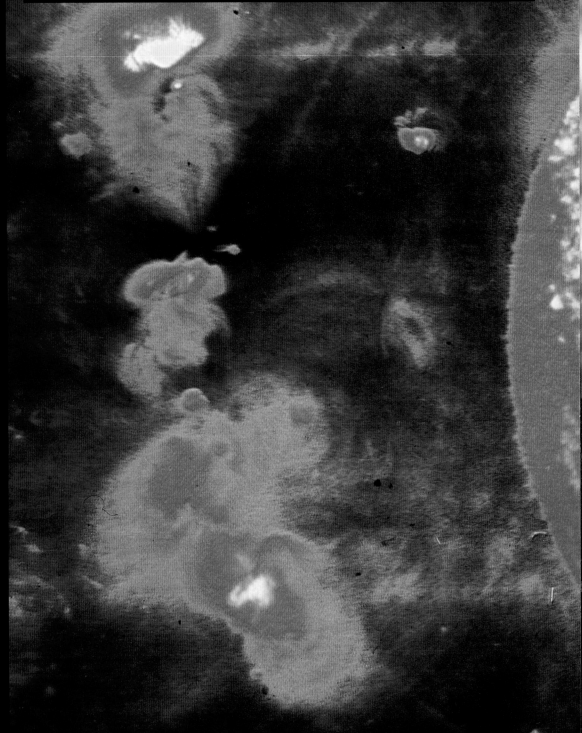

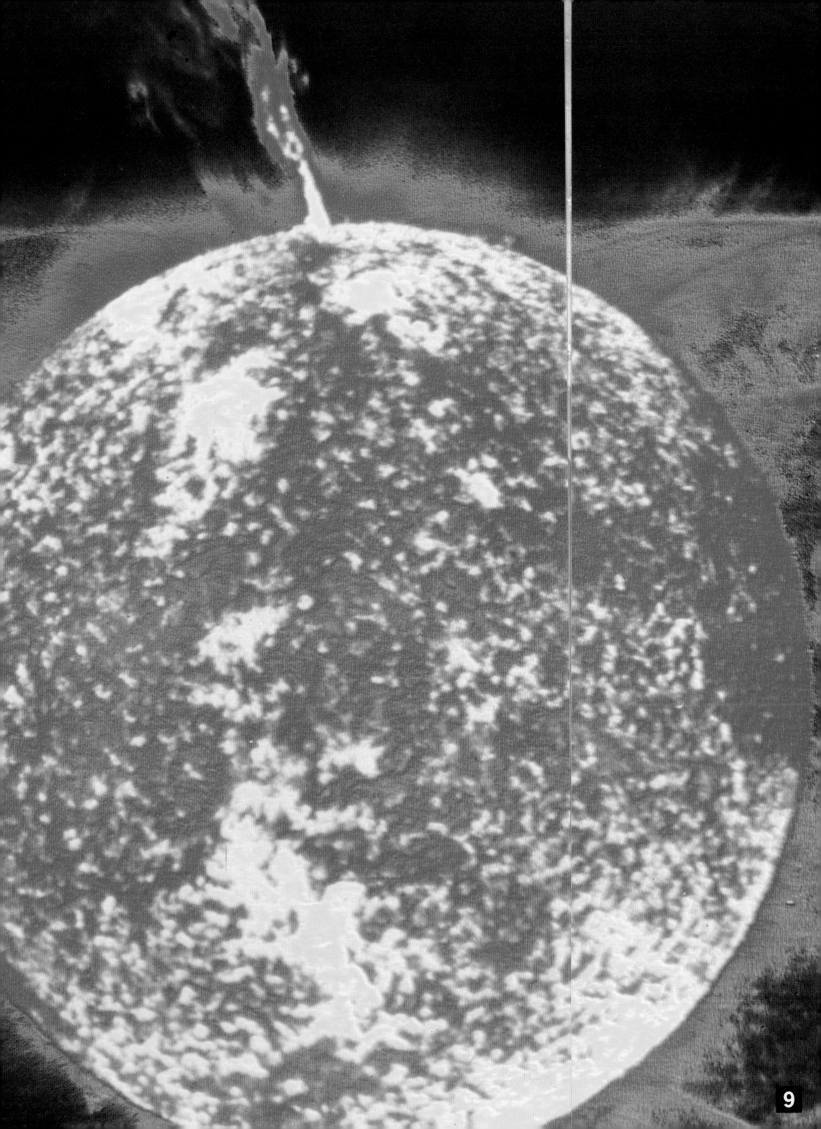

9

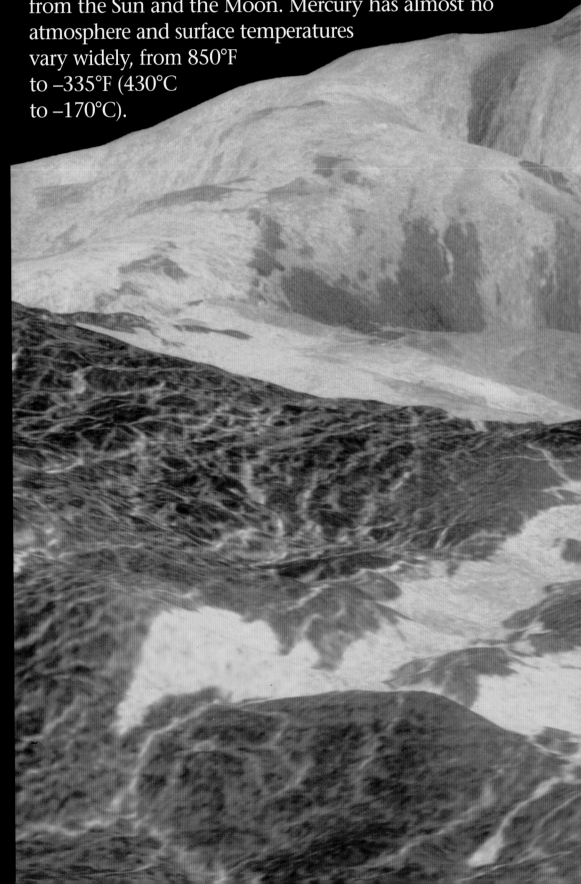

MERCURY AND VENUS

ercury and Venus are the closest planets to the Sun. Both are sometimes visible in the eastern sky just before sunrise and in the western sky shortly after sunset. Mercury is hard to see, but Venus, when it appears, is the brightest object in the sky, apart from the Sun and the Moon. Mercury has almost no atmosphere and surface temperatures vary widely, from 850°F to –335°F (430°C to –170°C).

MERCURY

Mercury is the second smallest planet, and is only slightly larger than our Moon. The nearest planet to the Sun, it takes just 88 Earth days to complete an orbit. The planet spins on its axis very slowly, taking 59 days to complete one rotation. As a result, a day on Mercury lasts about 176 Earth days. This means that a Mercurian day is more than twice as long as an Earth year!

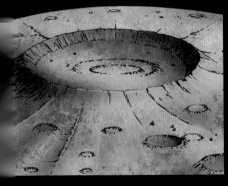

The surface of Mercury is dotted with craters made by meteorites that hit over 4 billion years ago.

Mercury has a very large, dense metal core. It occupies about 75 percent of the planet's radius. Above, there is a rock mantle covered by the thin crust.

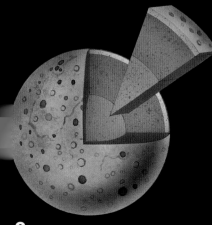

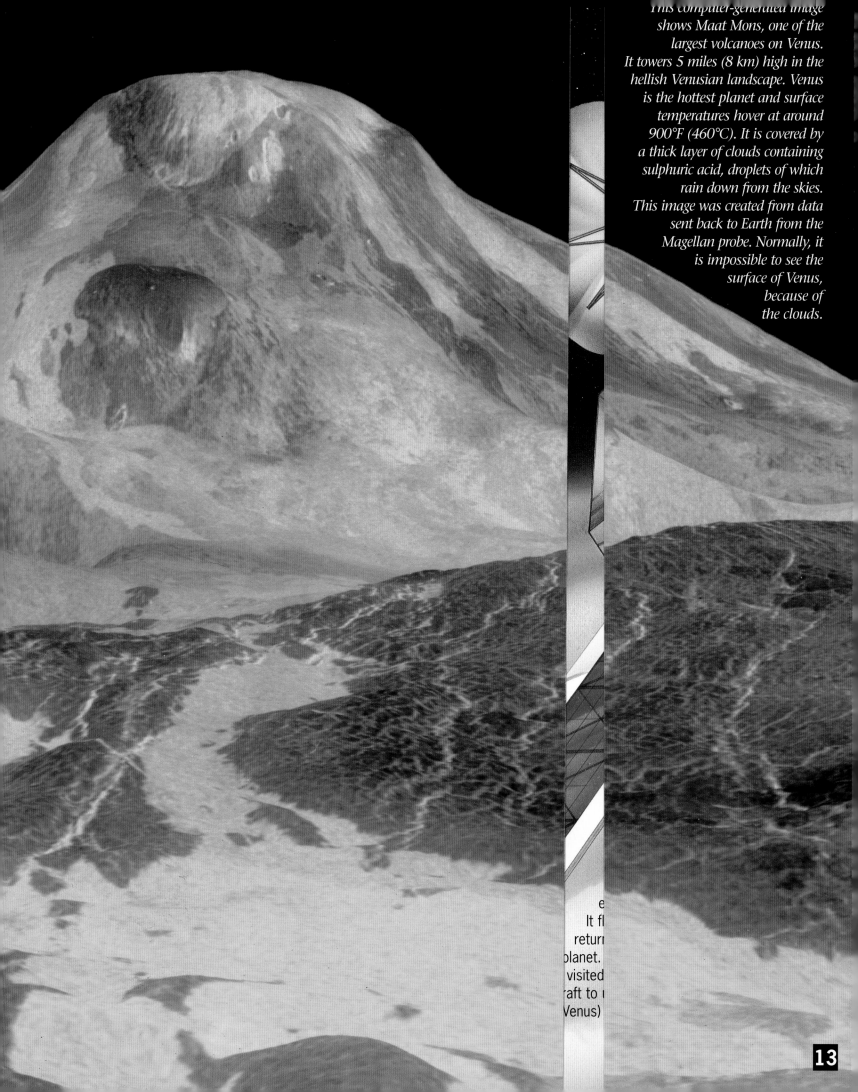

This computer-generated image shows Maat Mons, one of the largest volcanoes on Venus. It towers 5 miles (8 km) high in the hellish Venusian landscape. Venus is the hottest planet and surface temperatures hover at around 900°F (460°C). It is covered by a thick layer of clouds containing sulphuric acid, droplets of which rain down from the skies. This image was created from data sent back to Earth from the Magellan probe. Normally, it is impossible to see the surface of Venus, because of the clouds.

e
It fl
retur
planet.
visited
raft to
Venus)

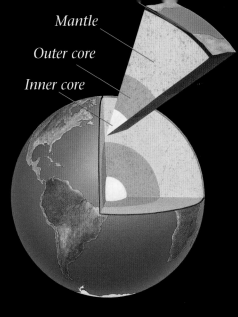

Mantle

Outer core

Inner core

STRUCTURE OF THE EARTH

The Earth has a thin outer crust over its solid rocky mantle. The inner core is composed of solid iron, while the outer core is molten (hot liquid) iron.

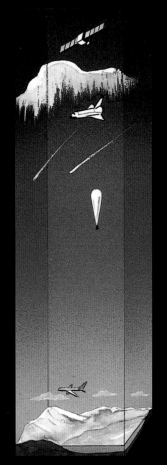

THE ATMOSPHERE

THE EARTH AND THE MOON

The Earth is third in line from the Sun, and the largest and densest of the four rocky, inner planets. Its atmosphere shields the surface from harmful radiation from the Sun and helps maintain relatively constant temperatures. The Earth's surface temperature varies between about –190°F and 136°F (–88°C and 58°C). Life on Earth is dependent on the oxygen in the atmosphere, which is produced by plant life. The Earth is the only planet known to support life. It has one large natural satellite, the Moon.

As this satellite photograph shows, the Earth's main physical features – the oceans, continental landmasses, and polar ice caps – are clearly visible from space. On most days about half of the planet is covered by clouds. The Earth is unique in being the only planet in the Solar System to have liquid water on its surface. More than 70 percent of the planet is covered by oceans.

cid

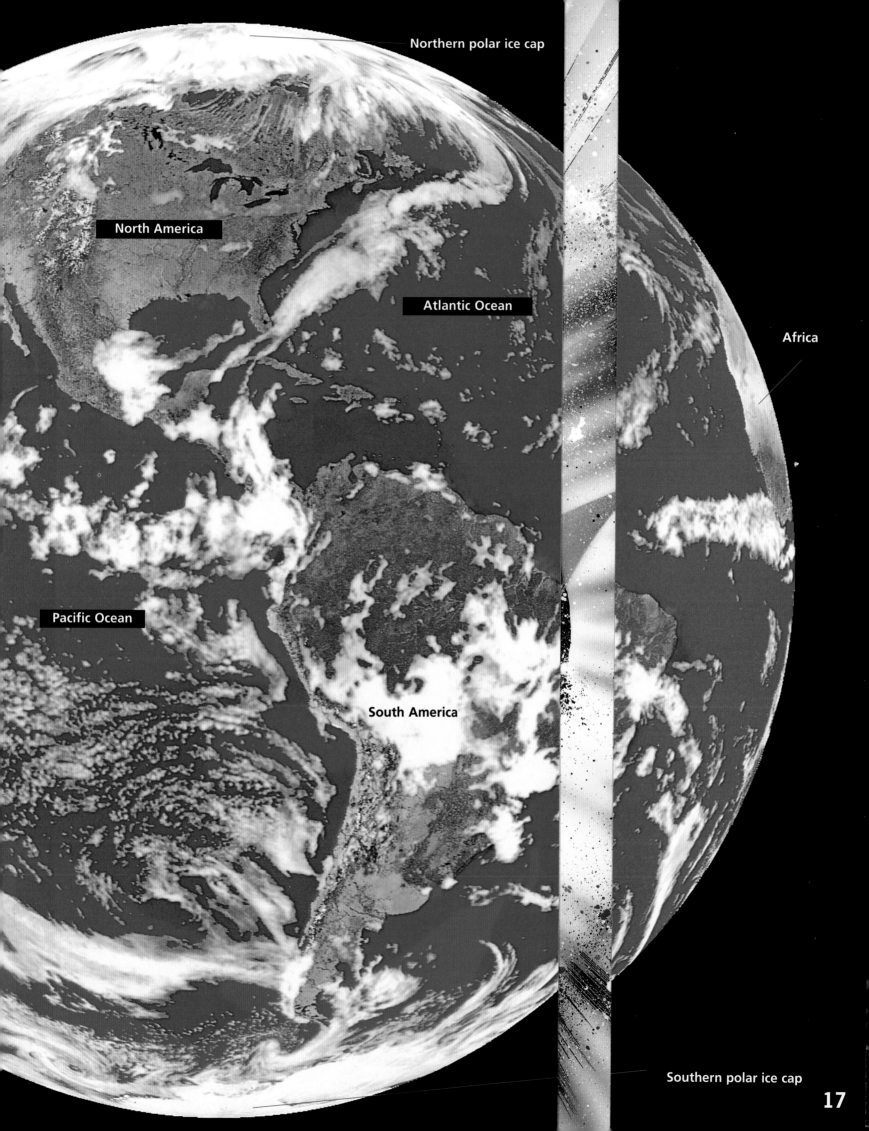

Northern polar ice cap

North America

Atlantic Ocean

Africa

Pacific Ocean

South America

Southern polar ice cap

17

LANDING ON MARS

Mars Pathfinder was the first craft to land on Mars in over 20 years. Using an unorthodox parachute-landing technique (see below), it touched down on July 4, 1997. When safely landed, it released the six-wheeled *Sojourner*, which spent nearly 3 months analyzing Martian rocks before the battery went flat.

1. At 5.8 miles (9.3 km) from the surface, Pathfinder's parachute opens.

2. Lander lowered. Radar active at 1 mile (1.6 km) from the surface.

3. Airbags inflate 10 seconds before landing. Braking rockets begin at six seconds.

4. Pathfinder bounces more than 15 times before rolling to a halt.

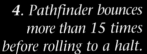

5. Airbags are deflated and retracted.

MARS

Mars is the fourth and last of the inner rocky group of planets. It is slightly further away from Earth than Venus, but has always excited human interest. For a long time astronomers thought that they could see evidence of life on Mars. But when the first space probes explored the planet with flybys in the 1960s and landings in the 1970s, it was discovered to be dusty, barren, and riddled with craters rather like those on the Moon. Nevertheless, the 1997 Pathfinder landing was followed closely by millions of people around the world. New exploratory missions are planned early in the 21st century.

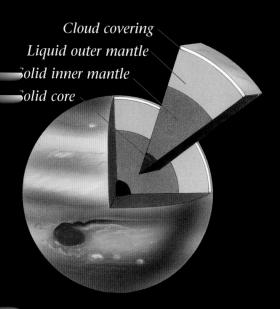

Cloud covering
Liquid outer mantle
Solid inner mantle
Solid core

STRUCTURE

Jupiter's thin covering of stormy clouds covers an outer mantle composed of hydrogen and helium. An inner mantle of metallic hydrogen is believed to cover a rocky core.

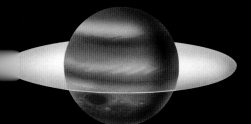

JUPITER'S RING SYSTEM

A photo taken by *Voyager 1* as it flew by Jupiter in 1979 revealed that, like the other gas giants, Jupiter also has a ring system. The very delicate rings are made up of particles of dust.

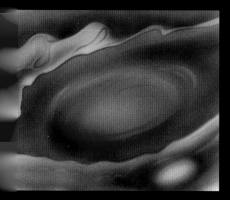

THE RED SPOT

Jupiter's surface is studded with over 1,000 swirling storm systems. The Red Spot (above) is the largest of these. This vast storm could engulf two whole planets the size of the Earth.

Jupiter has about 14 bands of dark-colored low pressure systems, called belts, circulating in the same direction as the planet rotates. It has just as many light-colored high pressure systems, called zones, moving in the opposite direction. When the two systems meet, vast swirling storm systems develop.

JUPITER

The first of the gas giants, Jupiter is the largest and most massive planet in the Solar System. Its diameter is 11 times that of the Earth, and its globe could contain about 1,300 planets the size of ours. Despite its huge dimensions, Jupiter spins on its axis once every 9 hours and 55 minutes. This very rapid rotation causes the planet to bulge at the equator and also whips up very strong winds that stretch its cloudy atmosphere into the long parallel bands of swirling color that characterize the planet's appearance.

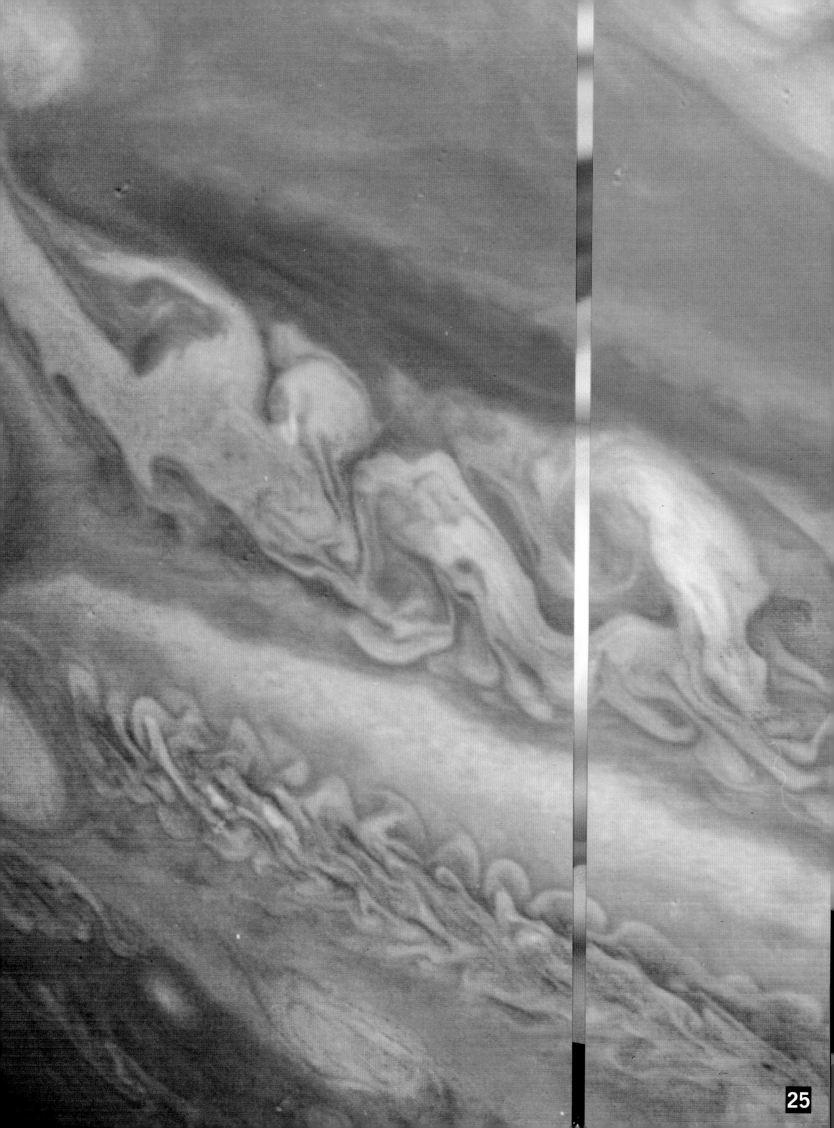

25

Saturn has 18 named moons. A further five or six have also been identified. At 3,219 miles (5,150 km) in diameter, Titan is the largest (and the second largest in the Solar System, after Jupiter's Ganymede). Saturn's most distant moon, Phoebe, is almost 8.1 million miles (13 million km) from the planet.

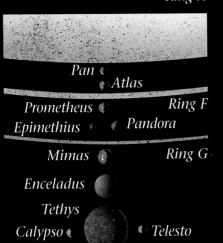

Ring A

Pan
Atlas
Prometheus   Ring F
Epimethius   Pandora

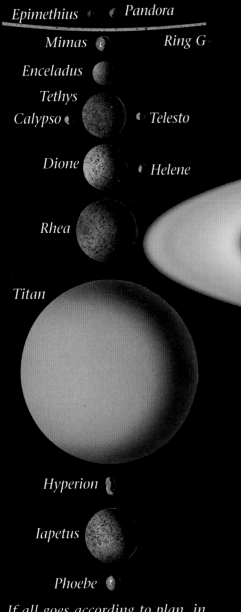

Mimas   Ring G
Enceladus
Tethys
Calypso   Telesto
Dione   Helene
Rhea
Titan
Hyperion
Iapetus
Phoebe

If all goes according to plan, in November 2004 the Huygens *probe will be released on Titan from the* Cassini *Saturn orbiter. Once landed, it will measure the moon's temperature and composition.*

SATURN

After Jupiter, Saturn is the second largest planet in the Solar System. It is the sixth farthest from the Sun. Like the other gas giants, it is composed mainly of hydrogen and helium. Saturn spins very rapidly and a day lasts for just 10 hours and 39 minutes. Very strong winds blow in Saturn's atmosphere, sometimes reaching speeds of 1,000 miles (1,600 km) per hour. Beneath the planet's high yellow clouds, a vast white storm system is sometimes visible. But the most striking thing about Saturn, which has intrigued astronomers for over 300 years, is the planet's ring system.

E F

ere
om
ron
sev
up
, so
ngs
th
forr
on c
gra
e le
rme

This infrared image taken from the Hubble Space Telescope *shows how Saturn is visibly flattened at the poles due to the speed at which it rotates. Two fierce storm systems can be seen in the pink area near the planet's equator.*

NEPTUNE'S CLOUDS

Methane rises through the atmosphere on Neptune to form high altitude clouds. Violent winds blow at over 1,250 miles (2,000 km) per hour. The most striking feature is a huge dark storm system, known as the Great Dark Spot.

High methane cirrus clouds.

Sunlight turns the methane into hydro-carbon snow, which falls then rises again as methane.

STRUCTURE

Uranus and Neptune are similar in structure. Both have atmospheres of hydrogen, helium, and methane gases, merging into dense mantles made of ice, ammonia, and methane. Their solid, rocky cores are also similar.

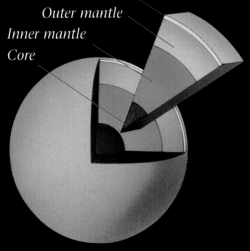

Atmosphere

Outer mantle

Inner mantle

Core

The traces of methane in the atmosphere of both planets gives them their characteristic blue-green color.

URANUS AND NEPTUNE

Uranus and Neptune are the third and fourth gas giants and the seventh and eighth planets from the Sun, respectively. All of the inner planets and Jupiter and Saturn are visible to the naked eye and have been known since ancient times. Uranus was discovered by William Herschel in 1781 with the aid of a telescope. Neptune was discovered by prediction in 1846 after astronomers observed that Uranus' orbit was being affected by its neighbor's gravitational forces.

Uranus and Neptune maintain an average distance of about 1,800 million miles (2,900 million km) and 2,800 million miles (4,500 million km), respectively. A Uranian year (the time it takes the planet to complete one orbit of the Sun) lasts for 84 Earth years. A year on Neptune lasts for 164.8 Earth years!

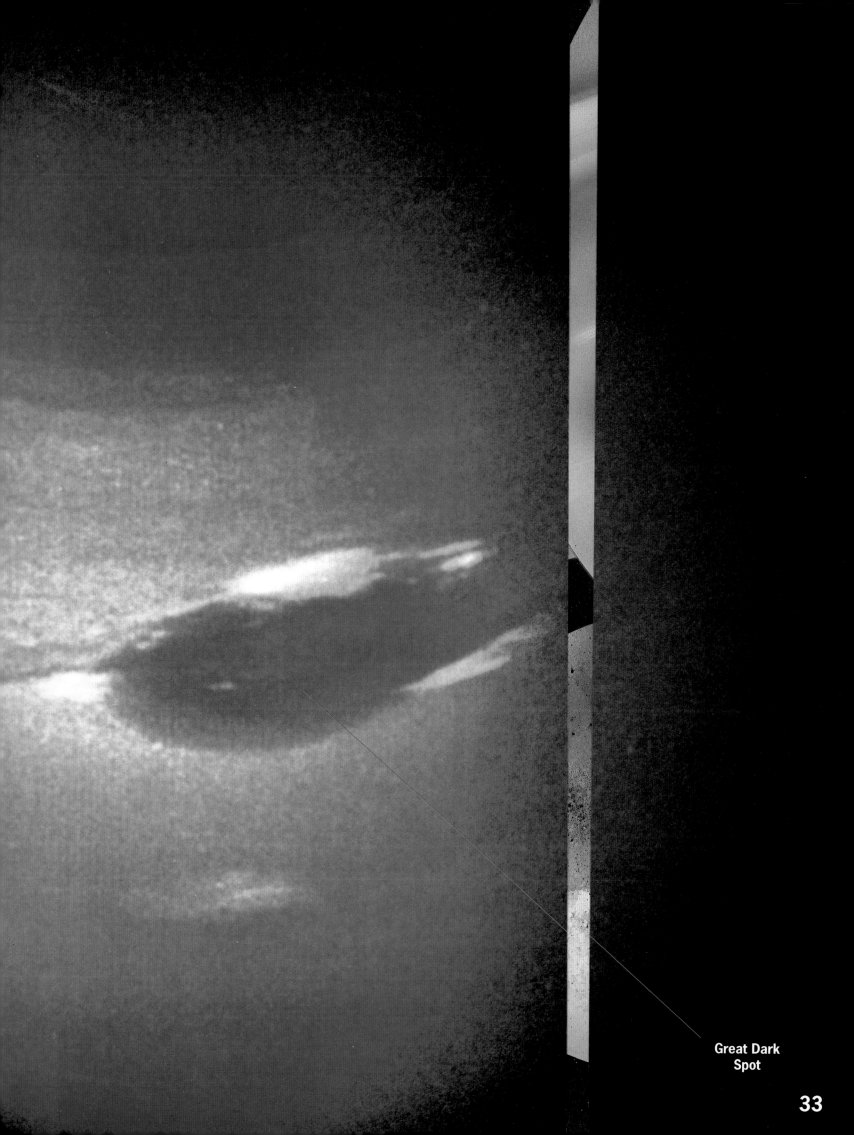

**Great Dark
Spot**

PLANET X

Many astronomers believe that a tenth planet lies waiting to be discovered at the very fringes of our Solar System. Pluto was discovered by prediction when scientists were seeking an explanation for the discrepancies in Uranus' orbit. Pluto is too small to account for them all. The search continues...

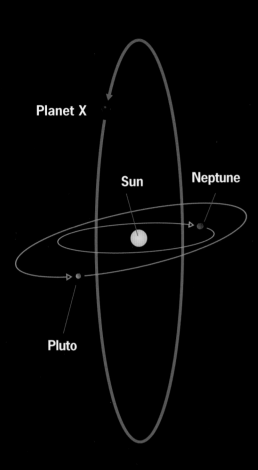

Some people think that Planet X will be found in an orbit at right angles to the other planets.

Pluto

STRUCTURE OF PLUTO

Pluto (right) is denser than the four gas giants and their moons. Astronomers believe that it has a large, rocky core wrapped in a thick layer of ice, frozen methane and nitrogen. Pluto's thin atmosphere is composed of nitrogen and methane.

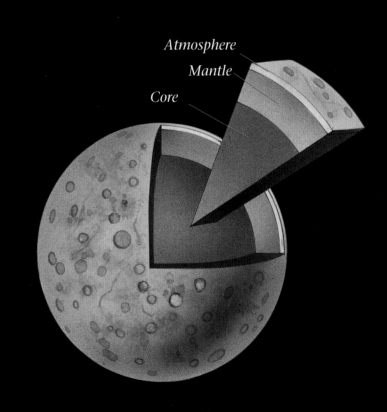

Atmosphere

Mantle

Core

36

PLUTO

During most of its 248-year orbit, Pluto is the farthest planet from the Sun. However, its elliptical orbit brings it inside Neptune's for 20 years of each orbit. Pluto keeps an average distance of 3.75 billion miles (6 billion km) between itself and the Sun. Measuring just 1,437 miles (2,300 km) in diameter, Pluto is the smallest and also the least massive planet in the Solar System. It is a rocky planet, probably covered with ice and frozen methane. Pluto has just one known satellite, Charon, which was discovered in 1978. Charon is large for a moon, at half the size of its planet. Because they are quite similar in size, Pluto and Charon are often considered to be a double-planet system.

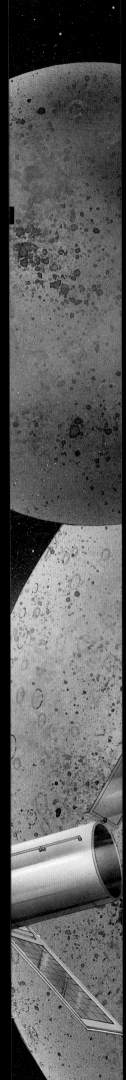

Charon is believed to be almost identical in structure to its parent planet, Pluto.

Charon

Due to their extreme distance from Earth, Pluto and Charon are the least well known and visited planetary groups in the Solar System. No flybys or landers have reached either. The image on this page was taken by the Hubble Space Telescope.

INDEX

PICTURE CREDITS

The Publishers would like to thank the following for providing photographs and for permission to reproduce them: